AF374813

God is the Creator
Of every single thing.
This knowledge brings joy–
That it's all from the King.

TA-DA

God's Creation Story in Rhyme
Copyright © 2026 by Mary Ann Hoffman

Softcover ISBN: 979-8-9939968-0-6
Hardcover ISBN: 979-8-9939968-1-3

Library of Congress Control Number: 2026904025

Illustrations by Julia Dell Otterness
Cover and Interior Design by Emily Almendariz

Ta-Da
by Mary Ann Hoffman
1

In the very beginning

there was nothing but dark.
Nothing could pierce it—
Not even a spark.

Over dark waters
God's Spirit hovered
Like a mother eagle
Who keeps her nest covered.

2

Then Papa God's voice,
Like a great sonic boom,

Pierced through the
darkness
And scattered the gloom.

"LET THERE BE
LIGHT!"

And there was light!
He called the light
"day"
And the darkness
was "night."

TA-DA!

Then PAPA divided
the waters just so-

With blue skies above
The blue seas below.

TA-DA!

He made deserts and beaches
With miles of sand,
And plants and tall trees
To cover the land.

He commanded the plants
To bear fruit and seeds.
He knew their abundance
Would meet future needs.

So many gorgeous flowers—
Tulips, lilies, daffodils.
He spoke and created
Canyons, waterfalls and hills.

TA-DA!

8

Then: "I'll create planets,
Multi-colored stars so bright,
Brilliant golden sun to rule the day,
Silver moon to rule the night."

"What will be next?"
Curious angels wondered.

TA-DA!

The angels jumped in surprise
When at His mighty words
The sky was filled up
With all kinds of birds!

Joyfully soaring,
Winging in flight,
Flapping and chirping
In new-found delight:

Tiny minnows swimming,
Giant whales with spouts,
Dolphins, starfish, sharks
And shiny rainbow trouts.

Penguins and ostriches
And peacocks, too,
Couldn't fly, but explored
Their land which was new.

The rivers and streams
And oceans were filled
With amazing creatures
As Papa God willed.

God saw that it was good,
And the creatures were
blessed.
The angels were eager
To see what came next.

TA-DA!

Land-dwelling creatures
were next in God's work,
All kinds of animals, with many a quirk.

12

Bunnies with cottontails,
Lions who roar,
Kangaroos with pockets
And so many more!
Gorillas and chimpanzees,
Elephants with trunks,
Graceful striped tigers
And smelly black skunks.

Fireflies and ladybugs,
The grasshopper who jumps,
Doggies and kitty cats
And camels with humps.
He created more and more,
And made the angels laugh
As He made the platypus
And the long-necked giraffe!

Since there is no limit
To God's creativity,
The angels must have wondered,
"What else will we see?"

13

Then Papa God smiled
At what was to be…
"I will now make mankind
In the image of Me!"
The angels rejoiced
In seeing His bliss,
Amazed that the Holy God
Would do something like this!
This was the greatest
Creation He'd done—
His own human family—
A daughter and son.

God blessed them and told them
To rule over the earth,
And fill it with others
Through the giving of birth.

TA-DA!

15

Each person born
Was perfectly planned.
They came from Papa's heart
And His wonderful hand.

People here
And people there,
With different shades
Of skin and of hair.

People with brown and green,
Blue and hazel eyes;
Each person unique
In features and size.

Every child born
A fine piece of art.
God's breath was in them
Right from the start.

TA-DA!

TA-DA!

TA-DA!

So listen and know…
It's so very true…
He wanted MANY
And… especially you!

You were handcrafted
By His unique design;
Brought to this earth
For this special time.

When you were born,
When the perfect time came,
He whispered with gladness
Your marvelous name.

A SPECIAL BLESSING PRAYER

Papa God's voice tells you,
"You're a child extraordinaire;
In NO way a mistake:
Created with great care.
"My spark of life is in
The center of your heart,
I have TREMENDOUS plans for you,
And will help you do your part.
"Just know, my precious one,
You are my dearest dear.
Anytime you feel alone,
Don't forget, I'm always near.
"Just be very still
And listen for My love.
It comes in many ways
From around you and above!
"You are my favorite one;
A treasure so grand.
Before time existed
I had you planned!"

Acknowledgments

A round of applause goes to You, God! We honor the magnificence of Your creative handiwork.

Thanks to Jackie Macgirvin and her friend Kathy Burris whose touches turned TA-DA into poetic art.

Julia, you tuned your listening ear to the heartbeat of Papa-God and changed the blank canvas into vibrant life! Thank you for hours of sitting in His Presence.

Emily, like a master weaver, you've brought all the pieces together!

A special thanks to my dear friend Gloria who lives now in the great cloud of witnesses. Her vision-dream ultimately led me to this first volume of TA-DA.

Like the stars in the sky and the sand on the seashore, there is no way to count those who helped in the shaping of the story. Thanks all. We did it. We truly are better together.

May you the reader, experience God our Father's love for you and be filled with His Son, Jesus Christ Who "is the same yesterday, and today and forever." Hebrews 13:8

Author Bio

Mary Ann Hoffman loves to encourage others by planting seeds of hope that help them grow in our Father's beautiful Garden.

Wherever she goes, her message remains the same: "My home is in my Father's Heart." She believes Papa God sees each one of us and holds us as His treasure close to His Heart.

In addition to a Bachelor's degree in Early Childhood Education (UMSL), Mary Ann holds Master's degrees both in Counseling (UMKC) and Theology (Dominican House of Studies).

She has traveled extensively doing missions work and educational workshops in the USA, Cyprus, El Salvador and the Great Barrier Island.